Animal parenting

TONY SEDDON

Facts On File Publications
New York, New York • Oxford, England

Library of Congress Catalog Card Number:

88-045742

Designed and produced by BLA Publishing Limited,
East Grinstead, Sussex, England.

A member of the **Ling Kee Group**
LONDON·HONG KONG·TAIPEI·SINGAPORE·NEW YORK

Phototypeset in Britain by BLA Publishing/Composing Operations
Printed and bound in Spain

10 9 8 7 6 5 4 3 2 1

Note to the reader
On page 59 of this book you will find the glossary. This gives brief explanations of
words which may be new to you. Answers to questions are given on page 58.

Contents

Males and females

In many animals it is easy to distinguish between males and females. The two sexes often have their own special shapes and colors to help in recognition. In other species like the giant panda it is hard to tell the sexes apart.

Sometimes being either male or female is not so straightforward. For example, oysters undergo periodic sex changes depending on the temperature of the water in which they live.

Coloring up

Color is important in the life of many animals, especially birds and fish. Male birds are often more brightly colored than females of the same species. A drab-looking female is camouflaged and has more chance of survival when sitting on the nest.

Apart from being brilliantly colored, some male fish can change color depending on their mood. A male moorish idol will actually become a brighter color when it meets another male out for a swim.

▲ Sometimes a male has to fight other males of the same species to win the right to breed. Size is important and so is the possession of weapons like antlers and tusks to help in fighting.

▶ The male peafowl has a magnificent long tail which he uses to help attract a female at the start of the mating season.

In many invertebrate species (animals without backbones) the female is bigger than the male. Female spiders are sometimes three times bigger than their partners. They are also much fiercer. In most birds it is the opposite, although in birds of prey the males are smaller. In mammals like lions and elephants, the male is always larger, stronger, and more powerful.

▲ In some butterflies the sexes look the same but in other species they are very different in shape and color. This is a pair of birdwing butterflies from New Guinea. Do you think that early explorers can be forgiven for not realizing they are male and female of the same species?

The male anglerfish is so small that it grows as a parasite on the much bigger female. In fact, the males are so small that a female can afford to have several attached to her at any one time. This very special relationship is an adaptation to the inky blackness of the ocean depths. It is hard for the sexes to find each other in the dark. Once they have met up, the small male makes sure he stays in contact by growing into the female's body. Eventually he becomes part of her.

◄ A queen termite is many times bigger than a king termite. Her enormously swollen abdomen is a large egg-laying machine which produces as many as 8,000 eggs every day of her life.

More about ⟫ Colours p 8-9, 28 Spiders p 19
Termites p 13, 55

Finding a mate

Most animals have developed ways of communicating to help find a mate. They make visual, sound, and chemical signals. It is usually the male that tries to attract the female and put her in the right mood for mating.

▲ Many animals have courtship displays which involve both of the animals. Crowned-cranes do an elaborate ceremonial dance. The wings are held out to show off the bold feather patterns and the birds strut about with plenty of bobbing and bowing of heads.

Love songs

Nocturnal animals and those living in dense vegetation use sound signals to help find the right mate. Crickets and grasshoppers chirp a high-pitched serenade by rubbing legs and wings together, and frogs and toads croak their night messages. The frog with the loudest voice wins his mate first.

Gibbons call in the jungle canopy and humpback whales sing long and complicated songs to keep in touch in the depths of the ocean. But light is sometimes a better signal than sound. This is why many deep-sea animals have light-producing organs while, on land, fire flies flash their coded messages in the night air.

Dressing up

Bright colors are very attractive and are often used in courtship and display. But they have to be seen to work properly so they are used mainly by day animals. Fish, reptiles, and birds often specialize in very colorful costumes but it is usually the males who wear them.

◀ Sometimes a male animal "colors-up" at the beginning of the breeding season to attract a female and to frighten off other males. This is why a male stickleback wears a red breast in spring.

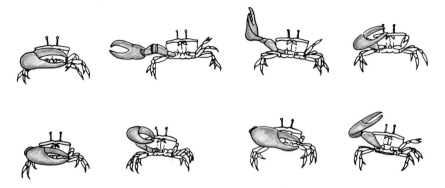

◄ Here are two species of fiddler crab. You can see that the one at the top makes a kind of beckoning or "come here" action with his huge claw. The other crab performs a salute. Each signal is designed to attract the right female to the male fiddler crab's burrow in the sand.

Flying the flag

Some animals inflate parts of their body or wave bits of themselves to attract a mate. The male frigate bird blows up a big red "throat balloon" while a male fiddler crab waves a big front claw like a colored flag. Each type of crab has his own distinctive kind of claw wave. Some male spiders flap their legs like a semaphore message to let the female know they have come to mate, not to be eaten!

Food parcels

It is common for male animals to give presents to females they hope to mate with. Some terns offer a fishy gift while a bird called the roadrunner hands over a tasty lizard to his mate-to-be. Some bower birds offer the female a gift once she has been enticed into his bower.

Male spiders have to take extra care. They find that a gift of food wrapped in silk distracts the female and makes her forget about wanting to eat him when mating starts.

Scent signals

Perfumes called pheromones are used by many animals in the quest to attract a mate. Some male moths carry huge feathery antennae to catch the scent of the female, often from a great distance.

Smells often tell a male if the female is ready to accept him. Female mammals come onto "heat" at certain times in the year. When this happens the male picks up scent signals from the female's body which tell him she is ready to mate. The male porcupine even urinates over his mate-to-be to tell other males to keep away.

◄ The brightly colored and swollen bottom of a female baboon signals to the waiting male that she is ready to accept him as a breeding partner.

More about ›› Colours p 6-7, Gibbons p 17, Sticklebacks p 28
Spiders p 19, Scent signals p 10-11 Baboons p 19, 54

9

Staking a claim

◄ Howler monkeys live in family groups of up to twenty animals. They announce that they are in residence by shouting to rivals who might be interested in trespassing. The red howler monkey can make itself heard over a distance of 3 miles (4.8 km).

Sniffing the air

Animals with big territories to patrol use scent as a signal. Smells have the advantage of hanging around for a long time, even after the "owner" has gone away. Mammals use the smell of their urine and droppings to stake their territorial rights. These scents send out their clear signals both day and night, telling other animals to keep their distance. Some animals like cats and dogs are "smelly territory claimers," so are antelopes and rhinoceroses.

Animals often have to use signals to advertize to other males and females that they are "at home." They use all kinds of signals including visual, sound, and smell. Many birds tell the world about themselves and their territories by singing from a high tree or post in the early morning in spring. Once they have made this announcement, the rest of the day can be spent in courting, nest building, or finding food for the young ones. However, the trouble with visual and sound signals is that the owner has to be present to show them off or produce them. They also work best only over a short distance.

▼ Male dogs leave their scent as high off the ground as possible. This helps it to evaporate more quickly. The smell also catches the wind more easily so it can be carried far and wide.

▲ Hippopotamuses use a muck-spreader technique to mark their boundary fences. The males squirt a liquid diarrhea. They spread their smelly message further by waving the tips of their tails in the spray like a paint brush. This is a good way of warning other hippopotamuses to "keep off."

Glands and scents

Antelopes leave dollops of scent all over the place. It is produced by two small glands, one in the front of each eye. Antelopes rub the thick, sticky substance produced by these glands onto twigs and branches as they walk along. The scent signals given off act as chemical messages to other antelope.

Rhinoceroses also plant scent around their territories but this time from glands on their feet. Hyaenas use a completely different technique. They rub their backsides along the ground and so spread the scent from small glands on their bottoms.

The bush baby lives in thick tropical vegetation. It cannot rely on accuracy to hit a leaf with its droppings or catch a twig with a squirt of urine. So, instead, it urinates over its hands and feet and then climbs about. It is a very efficient way for the bush baby to spread its smelly message on anything it touches.

More about 〉〉 Scent signals p 8-9

All kinds of homes

Many animals do very well without a home but others need the safety of a den or nest. A home is a special part of an animal's territory where it can find shelter and protection and in which it can breed and bring up its offspring. Some homes are very simple, perhaps only a hollow in the ground. Others are very complicated structures, both large and small. Some are used for only a few days or weeks. Others are more or less permanent.

Holes in trees

Holes in trees are a favorite place to set up home in. Birds like woodpeckers dig a hole themselves but other animals like marmosets and other small mammals take up residence when the original owner has moved out. Animals swop homes quite often!

Tree holes make very safe homes in which to rear a family, especially if the entrance is too small for predators to enter. They are also warm and dry because they are sheltered from the wind and rain.

▶ Birds make all kinds of nests using many different building techniques. Some sew, others work like potters, carpenters, and engineers. This huge nest belongs to the social weaver bird. More than 50 pairs of birds nest in this big communal home.

▲ The female harvest mouse builds her small nest all by herself, a few days before she gives birth. The nest has no entrance so mother and babies burrow through the wall when they want to enter or leave.

◀ Beavers are skilled engineers. They build complicated dams and lodges using trees they have cut down with their sharp teeth. The babies are brought up in safety, inside the lodge. Young beavers are extra safe because the entrance and exit to the lodge is underwater.

Some termite homes are enormous structures housing two million insects. The offspring are kept in conditions where the temperature and humidity are carefully controlled by an ingenious air-conditioning system.

A hole in the ground

Many animals live under the ground. Some spiders and insects burrow as do certain frogs, lizards, and snakes. Birds like shearwaters and puffins nest underground but they take over disused rabbit burrows in which to lay their eggs and rear their young.

Burrowing mammals usually dig their own tunnels and galleries but some like to make a take-over bid. Cape hunting dogs often use the disused holes of aardvarks during the breeding season.

Mammals like rabbits and badgers dig very complicated homes which are able to house many individuals. A badger set may contain twelve or more animals and a rabbit warren even more.

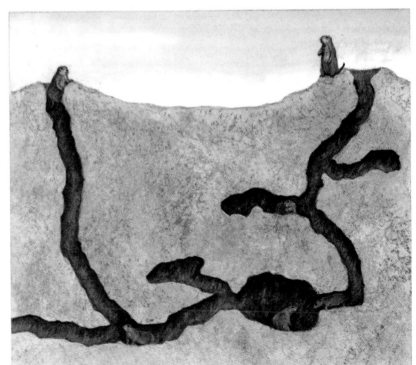

▲ Prairie dogs build huge towns under the ground. Adult females each have their own nesting chamber where the babies are born and reared. After weaning, the young spend more time playing in the galleries and on the surface, under the watchful eye of a guard.

More about ≫ Tree holes p 55 Rabbits p 39
Prairie dogs p 15, Termites p 7, 55

Getting to know you

Adult animals do not always get on with each other when they first meet, even males and females get worried. However, animals living in family groups need to know how individuals feel about each other.

In the case of the two sexes, it is important for males and females to get along if they are going to breed successfully. They must be able to show that they are friendly and interested in each other. Animals have various ways of doing this, just like humans. They cuddle and touch, give presents and even "kiss" each other in some cases. Later, this kind of behavior may develop into proper courtship and display rituals between males and females.

▲ This flightless cormorant lives on the Galapagos Islands in the Pacific. When a bird comes back to the nest to take over sitting duties, it brings a piece of seaweed as a gift. If the returning partner does not have a present to give, it quickly gets sent away. Other animals give gifts, including spiders.

◀ Horses greet each other by pulling back their lips and showing their teeth. It looks a bit like a threat but it isn't. When saying "hello" horses keep their ears pricked up. They lie flat against the head when threatening each other.

► Elephants often behave very affectionately towards each other. When two elephants meet they touch trunks and rub shoulders. Sometimes they even touch trunk tips almost as if they are kissing. It is actually a "nose kiss." They may just stand close to each other for a long time. It is a "getting to know you" piece of behavior.

▲ Prairie dogs live in large groups in underground burrows. When two animals meet each other for the first time they "kiss" to find out if they are from the same group. They are probably sniffing each other very carefully to catch each other's scent.

Hello duck!

Ducks meeting for the first time on a pond usually take a drink, so long as they are not trespassing on each other's territory. This is a greeting ceremony and a sign of peace.

When a male duck courts a female before mating, he performs a similar ritual. But this time he may use a kind of "shorthand." He only pretends to touch the water with his beak. Even so, his potential mate quickly gets the message.

Chimpanzees often shake hands and touch each other's faces. Mothers and babies often behave like this. But the closest type of greeting is a proper hug, often between male and female. Chimpanzees even make different faces to tell other chimps how they feel.

More about 〉〉 Courtship p 16, 18-19, 28 Presents p 9
Elephants p 55 Prairie dogs p 13

Couples and colonies

Many different kinds of relationships are formed by animal parents. Sometimes new pairs of animals come together at the beginning of each season, after the males have established territorial rights. Once the young have been raised and the breeding season is over, each parent will probably find a new partner the following year.

Till death us do part

Some animals pair for life — it is a kind of "marriage". Geese, swans, penguins, gibbons, and albatrosses do this. Marriage has its advantages. The parents do not have to waste time finding a new partner at the beginning of each year. Instead, they can get down to the serious business of having babies almost right away.

Other extremes

Animals like polar bears split up soon after mating and the female is left to bring up the babies by herself. But others, like lions, wolves, and apes, form small family groups in which to rear the young.

▶ Kittiwakes usually pair up for life. But sometimes the partnership does not work out properly. If a pair is unsuccessful during a breeding season, they "divorce' and try again next year with a new partner.

▲ Young albatrosses keep company for several years before finally mating. It is a kind of "engagement" during which time they practice the different courtship dances. This helps cement their partnership. This is important because albatrosses pair for life, once the decision is made.

Gibbons mate for life. They form small family groups with their own special territory. When the young are mature and ready to leave home their parents help them establish their piece of territory. Gibbons compete strongly for space in the rain forest canopy. An orphaned young male would have little chance of getting his own territory against other gibbons supported by their parents.

The colonial life

Many species of seabird live together in crowded colonies. The small island of St. Kilda is home for over a hundred thousand gannets. Colonial living makes finding a mate fairly easy but it also bring its problems. Parents have to recognize their eggs and babies, and there are always the problems of competition for food and overcrowding. A closely-packed colony is a dangerous place for eggs and chicks left alone, even for a moment. Adult gannets will not hesitate to kill unguarded chicks. Before leaving the nest, one of the gannet parents does a sky-pointing dance to tell the other parent to stay behind on guard. If both of them want a break, they argue about who goes first until one gives up.

▲ Seals and elephant seals rear their babies in colonies or rookeries. Each is made up of a number of harems, controlled by a large, dominant bull. Each male defends his territory and mates only with the females in his own harem. The pups are the result of a mating with another bull the previous year. They do not belong to the bull now in charge. His pups will be born in the next season.

More about ≫ Gibbons p 8-9
Courtship p 6, 8-9

The mating game

Packets of sperm

Many males produce packets of sperms which they give to their mates. Some, like crabs, stick their sac onto the female so that she can carry it around with her until her eggs are ready to be fertilized.

Other animals are more artful. Barnacles cannot move so the male produces an extra long sperm tube which he uses to place his sperms inside a female. The male giant octopus also transfers his sperms in packets. As you might expect, he has an extra large sperm sac. The female giant octopus receives a packet of sperms nearly 3 feet (1 meter) long.

If a pair of animals are going to produce their offspring successfully, the male's sperms must meet with the female's eggs so that fertilization can take place. Sometimes sperms and eggs are shed into water and their meeting is left to chance. But animals have also invented all kinds of ingenious ways to increase the chances of fertilization during mating.

▲ When two cuttlefish mate, the male places his sperm packet inside the female using a modified arm. A relative, the paper nautilus, goes a stage further. The male's special arm breaks off inside the female still clutching its valuable parcel of sperms.

▶ The male scorpion uses a clever trick when he mates. He wraps his sperms in a tiny packet which he leaves on the ground. Then he grabs his mate by her pincers and they start to dance. As he leads her over the parcel, the female picks it up to fertilize her eggs.

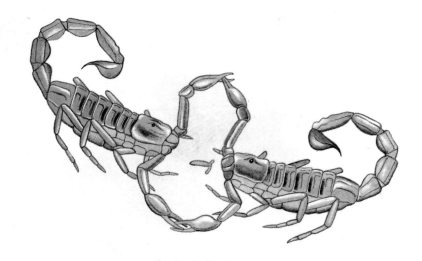

A male spider collects his sperms in a little silk pad which he then sucks into the hollow tips of his palps. These are tiny limb-like structures near his mouth. Now he is ready to mate. Approaching a female can be risky. He might be taken for a meal, not a mate! Some spiders tie the female down. Others, like tarantulas, hold her jaws apart. Whatever technique he uses, the male injects his sperms into the female spider like a doctor using a hypodermic syringe.

▼ In lions and tigers, the female often collapses during mating. The male sometimes get stuck in the female because of his extra-swollen penis. He can pull out only when it has returned to its normal size.

▲ Male birds do not have a penis. During mating the male and female reproductive openings line up and the sperms are squeezed from the male into the female.

Coming onto "heat"

For much of the year, a female mammal shows no interest in mating. It is only when she comes onto "heat" that she accepts a male as a breeding partner. Exciting smells tell the male about the female's condition. Female baboons even show off their brightly colored bottoms at this special time of year.

The male's penis ensures that fertilization has a good chance of taking place. It swells up with blood at the time of mating and the male uses it to shoot his sperms deep inside the female's body.

More about 〉〉 Sperms and eggs p 20-21, 22-23 Spiders p 7, 9
Lions p 51 Baboons p 9, 54

The start of a new life

The process of producing young is called reproduction. Some animals reproduce in a very simple way, while others have developed complicated techniques. Many single-celled animals like the amoeba simply divides into two separate cells. Each new cell is then able to live by itself.

▶ This is a single-celled animal called paramecium. You can see it is beginning to divide. Soon the two cells will separate and become individual animals.

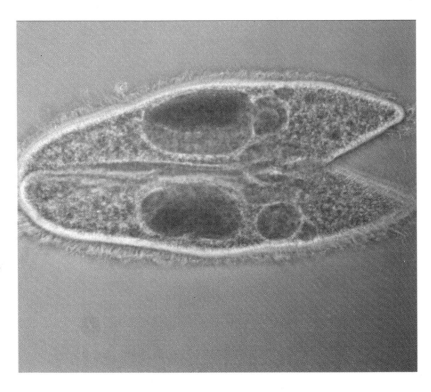

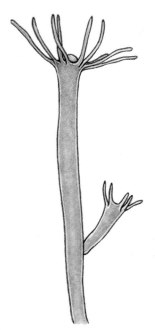

▲ This tiny animal called a hydra reproduces by budding. Little hydras grow out of the parent animal like small buds. Each becomes a miniature version of the adult. Each bud finally breaks off the parent hydra and moves away to live its own life.

Males and females

Bigger animals produce special sex cells called sperms and eggs. Animals like earthworms and snails are both male and female at the same time. They are hermaphrodite. More complicated animals like mammals and birds have separate sexes. The males produce sperms and the females eggs. Some animals like limpets and oysters and even some fish can also change sex. They switch from male to female and back again, depending on conditions.

Sperms and eggs

Sperms and eggs are the units of life. In some animals they are produced in enormous numbers, sometimes many millions. It is all to do with the chances of survival. Animals such as birds and mammals produce vast numbers of sperms but far fewer eggs. Therefore these animals have developed different kinds of reproductive techniques.

Fertilization is usually the starting point for any young animal. After it has taken place, the egg begins to develop and eventually becomes a new animal.

Blue prints for life

A fertilized egg contains all the information it needs for development. Half came from the male sperms and the other half was already in the egg which came from the mother. The information is in a kind of chemical data bank called genes, all carefully coded. Fertilization makes sure that a baby animal gets half its genes from its father and half from its mother. The genes control how the egg develops and what the new animal will look like.

▲ This baby guinea pig received some genes with faulty data. As it grew from the fertilized egg, it was not able to develop proper color. It was born an albino with white hair and pink eyes.

▼ Fertilization is always a risky business. Some animals avoid the problem by a kind of sex by-pass. Sometimes an egg will develop into a new animal without being fertilized. Greenflies can reproduce in this way. It is called parthenogenesis.

After fertilization

Fertilized eggs develop under different conditions. Many simply take their chances against enormous odds. Others are incubated in warm soil. In the case of birds, the parents incubate the eggs themselves. A fertilized mammal egg does something very different. It grows or implants into a part of the female's body called the womb. This is a kind of brood chamber where the baby can grow in safety. Some mammals can delay the implant. Then the offspring are born at the best time of year when it is warm and there is plenty of food about.

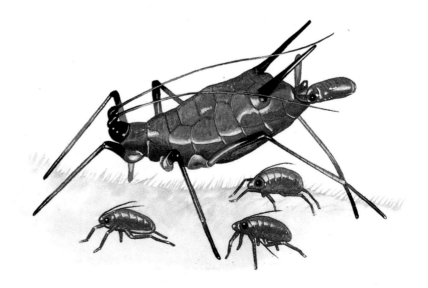

More about ⟫ Sperms and eggs p 18-19, 22-23
Males and females p 6-7

Against the odds

Fish eggs

The number of eggs laid by fish varies from species to species. The eggs of most fish are fertilized outside the female's body. This is a risky affair, so laying lots of eggs increases the chance of some of them becoming fertilized. At the other extreme, some sharks and rays lay only a few larger eggs. Big yolks and a tough outer covering help the eggs to survive.

◀ A female cockroach lays little packets, each containing sixteen tiny eggs. It has been worked out that one pair of cockroaches could have 164 billion descendants in just 7 months! But they do not. There is no parental care and most of the baby cockroaches are eaten by predators. Only a few in each generation survive to become breeding adults.

▼ At one spawning, a female ocean sun fish may lay as many as 300 million eggs. Probably fewer than five of these eventually become adults themselves.

Keeping up the numbers

Each kind of animal tends to produce enough offspring or eggs to keep its population numbers up. Some crabs produce two million eggs in every clutch and the common mussel squirts more than twenty million eggs into the sea in a single spawning. But these parents do not look after their eggs or their offspring. Most of them die or are eaten by predators. Only a handful of young survive to become adults themselves.

Other animals like birds and mammals produce fewer offspring. But in order to give their young a better chance of survival the parents take care of them during the early part of their lives. These animals show well-developed parental care.

Reptile nurseries

Most reptiles produce eggs although a few species give birth to live young. Some pythons lay as many as a hundred eggs which the female incubates with her shivering body to keep them warm. Crocodiles lay fewer eggs but they are extra good parents. They even carry their newly hatched babies to the safety of a nursery pool.

Bird's eggs

Clutch size in birds varies from species to species. The Emperor penguin produces a single egg which the male looks after and incubates in the depths of the Antarctic winter. Other birds like the South American rhea share one nest between several females and as many as 30 or 40 eggs are eventually incubated by a single male.

▲ Some frogs and toads lay hundreds of eggs. The giant toad from South America produces as many as 35,000 eggs in a breeding season. In these cases the eggs are left to develop by themselves so very few survive. Other types of amphibia are very good parents. These animals lay only a few eggs but they take great care of them and also the tadpoles which hatch out.

▼ In her lifetime, a female green turtle can lay as many as 2,000 eggs. There is no parental care and only a handful live long enough to breed.

Born alive

Female mammals have to carry their unborn young around with them. Because of this, they cannot afford to produce too many offspring at one go. So the birth of a single baby is quite common in many mammals. There are exceptions to this, and female mice may have twenty or more babies in a single litter.

The nine-banded armadillo breaks records in another way. A female always gives birth to identical quadruplets! But no matter how many babies in a litter, mammalian parents always look after their offspring until they are able to fend for themselves.

More about ⟫ Eggs p 18-19, 20-21 Nurseries and crèches p 44-45
Birds' eggs p 24-25, 27 Mammalian births p 38-39 Fish eggs p 27, 28

Bird eggs

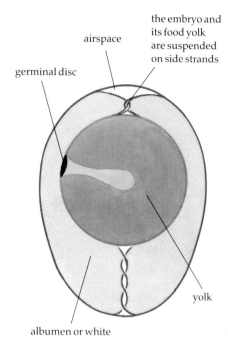

germinal disc

airspace

the embryo and its food yolk are suspended on side strands

yolk

albumen or white

Chicken's egg

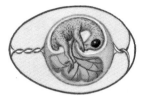

At 5 days the chick's heart already beats. It has blood vessels.

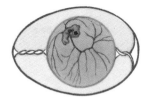

At 15 days the chick is recognizable as a bird.

At 20 days it is fully developed and will hatch next day.

▲ A bird's egg is a self-contained growth kit. The chick develops on top of a large food supply contained in the yolk. It lies surrounded by a watery egg white which works like a shock absorber and the whole egg is covered by a hard protective shell. The egg even carries its own air supply in an air space at one end. Growing up inside an egg is like living in your own private little pond.

Color and shape

Birds' eggs are often colored to help camouflage them and make it difficult for predators to spot them. Sand grouse nesting in desert regions lay very pale-colored eggs that match their background. Birds like oyster catchers produce mottled brown and black eggs to blend with the pebbly beaches on which they are laid.

Shape is also important. Eggs with a pointed end fit snugly into a nest with the points towards the center. This allows the parent birds to sit on them and incubate them more easily.

▲ A predatory gull looking for a tasty egg for breakfast would have to look twice before spotting this clutch of oyster catcher's eggs.

▲ Guillemots nest on rocky ledges. They lay conical-shaped eggs which roll in a circle. This prevents them rolling off the ledge into the sea. Guillemots do not muddle up their eggs. Each bird can recognize its own by their distinctive markings.

Egg care

Eggs need to be kept warm if they are to develop properly. Birds incubate their eggs using their own body heat. It is important to have a close contact between the parent's blood heat and the egg's shell. Many birds develop small patches of bare skin underneath called brood pouches. Each egg settles into its own pouch when the parent bird sits on the nest. Now the eggs are as close as they can be to the parent's body heat.

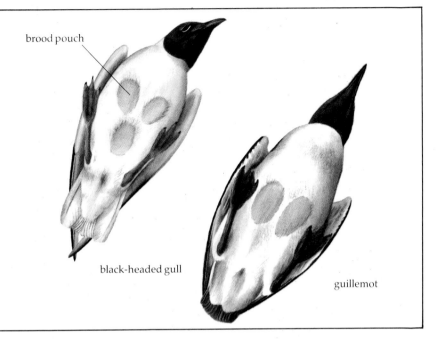

brood pouch

black-headed gull

guillemot

Giant eggs

The largest egg belongs to the ostrich, shown here about life size. An average egg weighs about 1.7 kg (3.7 lb). A female scrapes a shallow nest on the ground and then starts to lay her 10 or 12 eggs. Nests that contain more than 30 eggs are probably the result of several females using the same nest.

The male is the main incubator. He also gathers in any stray eggs. Female ostriches are not too fussy about where they lay!

Sometimes a female takes over the nursemaid's duties from the male. She usually does so during the day when her brown colours give her better camouflage. Often the eggs are left partly covered with sand in the daytime for the sun to keep warm.

Incubation lasts for about 40 days. The sturdy chicks need only a short rest before running off with their parents.

More about 》》 Clutch size p 23
Incubation p 23, 27

Egg watch

Different animals look after their eggs in different ways. Some hide them away and then visit them from time to time to make sure all is well. Others, like birds, keep in close contact on the nest and help them to hatch. Many animals also keep their eggs with them wherever they go. They are carried on backs, wrapped around legs, in the mouth and, in one case, even in the stomach. Nature has developed a great variety of "egg watch" programs.

▼ The female octopus hangs her eggs in a rocky cave and keeps watch over them. She cleans them regularly with her tentacles and flushes them with clean water.

▲ The female centipede "licks" her eggs to wash off any fungal spores which might attack them. Then she curls round them, to protect them from predators, before they hatch.

Male nursemaid

Some male giant water bugs carry the eggs on their backs. The females use a special kind of waterproof glue to stick them in position. Females are active fliers but egg-carrying males cannot get airborne with their heavy load of 30 or 40 eggs. Eventually the eggs hatch into tiny nymphs which then make their own way in the world.

Buried eggs

After the male mallee fowl has dug a deep pit, he fills it with plant material which he then covers with sand. As the vegetation starts to rot, it produces heat, just like a compost heap. When the female is ready to lay, her mate opens up his nest so she can place her eggs on the warm bed inside.

Now the male tends the nest carefully. He uses his beak and tongue like a thermometer to test its temperature. He continually adds or removes bits of the top covering to keep his "incubator" at 90°F (33°C). But he has a long wait and he is busy "gardening" for two months or more before the chicks hatch out.

sand

plant material

egg chamber

On guard

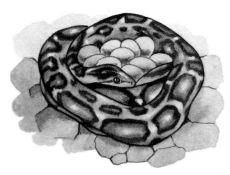

After laying a clutch of up to 100 eggs, a female python curls herself around them and remains on guard. She gives the eggs a daily shuffle so they can catch the warmth of the morning sun. If the temperature at midday gets too hot the female will also shade her eggs to cool them. If the temperature drops too low, she even shivers her body to warm the eggs up again. She only rarely leaves her eggs to catch a meal.

▲ At the time of spawning, the male labyrinth fish makes a bubble raft on the surface. Each egg laid by the female has its own built-in buoy — a tiny oil droplet. The eggs quickly float up to the raft where the male keeps guard until they hatch.

More about 〉〉
Frog and toad eggs p 30-31 Incubation p 25
Bubble rafts p 27, 28

Fish parents

▲ After a male stickleback has built his nest of weeds, he entices a female into it by leading her there with a zig-zag dance. His breeding colors not only attract the female but also help keep other males away from the nest.

The length of day and the temperature of the water tell many fish when it is time to breed. Most fish shed their eggs and sperms into the water. But this is a very risky way of going about things. This is why fish usually produce large numbers of eggs and sperms in the hope that some fertilization will take place.

Courtship

Some male fish build nests for the female to lay her eggs in. These males usually wear bright colors and perform a complicated dance to attract the female. Fish are very sensitive to vibrations in the water. African cichlid fish even beat small currents of water against each other's bodies when courting. They use these to exchange messages about how they feel towards each other.

Some fish take extra special care of their eggs. Gunnel or butterfly fish roll their eggs up into a ball as they are laid. Then one of the parents guards the eggs by curling its body around them. It may be that both parents act as caretaker.

▲ The eggs of the thorn-back ray are covered by a hard protective coat. Egg cases are often washed up on the beach after the babies have hatched. Dogfish produce similar eggs but anchor them to bits of weed to stop them floating away. Empty egg cases are sometimes called mermaids' purses.

The Siamese fighting fish has another technique. The male catches each egg in his mouth as it is laid and covers it in a slimy substance. He then places it in a raft of air bubbles which he built at the surface before mating.

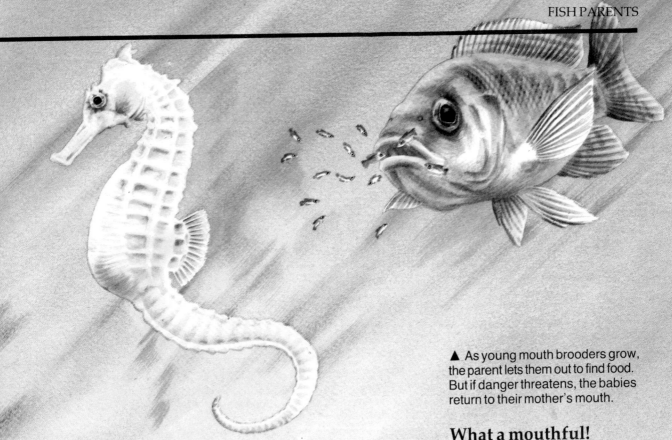

▲ As young mouth brooders grow, the parent lets them out to find food. But if danger threatens, the babies return to their mother's mouth.

What a mouthful!

Mouth brooder fish have an unusual way of looking after their offspring. The female snatches up her newly laid eggs before the male has had a chance to fertilize them. But all is not lost! The male has little egg-shaped dots on his anal fin near where he ejects his sperms. When the female fish tries to swallow these "pretend" eggs as well, she ends up with a mouthful of sperms "fired" at her by the male. The fertilized eggs now develop in the safety of the female's mouth. Five weeks later the babies are born. During this time, the female fish stops eating so that her eggs are never in danger of being swallowed.

Mussel power!

In the breeding season, the female bitterling fish grows an extra long egg-laying tube which she uses to place her eggs inside the shell of a freshwater mussel. At exactly the right moment, the male also injects his milt or sperms to fertilize the eggs inside the mussel's body. The eggs slowly develop in safety, protected by the mussel's shell. About four weeks later the eggs hatch and the baby bitterlings swim away, having avoided at least some of their enemies.

Male 'mothers'

In the seahorse it is the male who looks after the eggs, carrying them around in a special belly pocket for a month or so. Courting seahorses link tails and swim around close to the seabed. Eventually the female lays her eggs in the male's "pocket" where he fertilizes them. He then carries and protects them until the babies are born.

More about ⟩⟩
Courtship p 8-9, 16, 18-19
Bubble rafts p 27, 28

Frog parents

Amphibians show a wide range of parental care. Some, like the common frog, lay their eggs in water and then take no further interest in their development. Many of these eggs end up in the stomachs of fish and newts. Other amphibians, however, go to a great deal of trouble to protect their eggs and some even look after the tadpoles which hatch from them.

Both males and females can act as caretakers. Some push the fertilized eggs into little body pouches. Others have developed strange ways of behavior to make sure the offspring are well looked after. At least one type of frog actually swallows its eggs for safe keeping in its stomach!

A pygmy marsupial frog carries her eggs in an open bag on her back. When the tadpoles are ready to hatch, they are dropped into the water-filled hollows of a leafy plant.

▲ The male midwife toad carries strings of fertilized eggs wrapped around his back legs. Now and again he takes them back to a nearby pond to moisten them. Only when they are ready to hatch does he finally deposit them in water.

▶ Some arrow poison frogs lay their eggs on land and then keep watch until they hatch. The tadpoles then wriggle on to the parents' backs and are carried to water. Both males and females operate this taxi service.

Aquabatics

The Surinam toad from South America goes through a strange, tumbling mating dance during which the male places the fertilized eggs on the back of the female. Each egg quickly sinks through the female's skin and develops in its own little pocket on the female's back. After about 100 days, the tiny toadlets break out of their little cells and swim away to freedom.

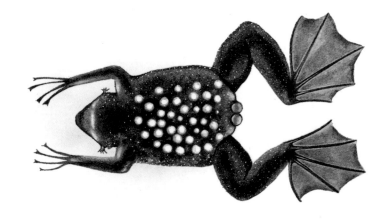

Living with father

The male Darwin's frog behaves in a very strange way. He takes about twenty new laid and fertilized eggs into his mouth and keeps them in a special throat sac until they hatch. Eventually, after a few weeks, the male coughs up a batch of tiny, but fully developed froglets.

A stomach full of babies

A rare little frog from Australia wins the title of the world's most unusual parent. When scientists first discovered the gastric-brooding frog, they could not believe their eyes when they saw a female "throwing up" lots of baby froglets. But this is how this frog looks after its offspring. It swallows its fertilized eggs and keeps them in its stomach until they have developed into miniature adults. Only then does it vomit them into the outside world. The babies are beautifully protected inside their mother. The female even "switches off" her stomach juices to prevent the tadpoles from being digested.

▲ Each female Surinam toad can carry about 100 eggs on its back. Each tiny developing tadpole uses its tail to get food from its mother's blood supply.

A "zip fastener" birth

The marsupial tree frog hatches out her fully-formed froglets from underneath a "zipper" fold in the skin down the middle of her back.

▲ A male Darwin's frog coughs up a tiny froglet.

More about 》 Arrow poison frogs p 45
Marsupials p 34-35

Feeding time

Eggs provide developing animals with plenty of food while they are inside. However, once the babies have hatched, they need to get food from somewhere else.

Sometimes the eggs are laid on top of a pile of food. Dung beetles lay their eggs on animal droppings, butterflies on leaves of plants, and flies on the bodies of dead and decaying animals. The offspring of these animals have a royal feast from day one! Other newly-hatched offspring may have to look for food themselves or, if they are lucky, it may be provided by the parents.

▲ Birds like chickens give their newly-hatched chicks very little help when it comes to feeding. However, they do point at tit-bits with their beaks to encourage the chicks to start pecking for food on the ground.

Food on tap

Baby birds and mammals are fed by their parents after they are born, sometimes for a long time. In the case of the baby elephant, the suckling time can last 3 or 4 years. Female mammals give their newborn babies lots of milk. There is food on tap! After the milk supply has dried up, the youngsters go on to other more solid foods.

Birds are hard-working parents, especially small ones like blue tits and wrens. They make lots of feeding trips to the nest, sometimes as many as 1,000 a day, in order to satisfy the hungry chicks.

Pigeon milk

Pigeons produce their own "milk" for their newly-hatched babies. They make this runny food substance in a part of the body called the crop. It is a thick, creamy fluid rather like syrupy cow's milk. It contains lots of fats and proteins to give the chicks a good start in life. After about 4 days, the "milk" is mixed with other things to get the chicks used to solid foods.

▼ The discus fish provides its young with a special kind of food. After the eggs are laid, both parents become coated with a slimy covering. It is rich in food, rather like milk. The newly-hatched babies attach to their parents and "graze" over their surface for a few days before going off to feed on their own.

Many young birds have brightly colored mouths to attract their parents at feeding time. The bright colors make obvious targets for the parents to push food into. A baby parrot finch even has two little pearly swellings at the corners of its beak. They work like tiny beacons, helping the parent birds to find the baby's mouth in the dark nest.

▼ A baby herring gull pecks at a bright red spot on its parent's beak. This signals to the parent to spit up food from its gullet to give the chick its dinner.

▲ Pelicans bring fish back to the nest for their young. The babies dive head first down into the parent's throat and help themselves to any partly digested fish they find there. Birds like gulls "throw up" lots of half-digested food for their offspring to feed on. Penguins do the same.

Water on the belly

It is also important for babies to get water. Young mammals drink milk from their mothers and so get their liquid this way. A bird called the roadrunner always gives its chicks a drink before feeding them. The sand grouse has developed a most unusual technique for supplying water to its babies. The male soaks his belly before returning to the nest. The babies drink from this built-in sponge.

More about

Milk p 40-41
Hens and chicks p 50

Platypuses and pouches

Many, but not all, female marsupials carry their young babies about in a pouch on the body. Baby marsupials are born after only a very short gestation time so when they leave the mother's body they are very tiny and helpless. They complete their development in the mother's pouch where they get warmth, protection and lots of milk.

Duckbills

The duckbill platypus is one of the world's strangest animals. It lays eggs like a bird but feeds its young on milk like a mammal. The female lays her two eggs at the end of a long tunnel in the bank of a river. She incubates them for two weeks during which time she never leaves the nest. When the babies hatch, they feed on the thick creamy milk which oozes out onto the mother's fur. By licking their mother's fur, the baby platypuses get enough milk to make them grow quickly.

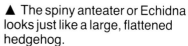

▲ The spiny anteater or Echidna looks just like a large, flattened hedgehog.

Prickly pouch

Just before a female spiny anteater starts to lay, she curls up so that she can drop her single egg into a small pouch on her tummy. The egg hatches after seven days and the baby then sucks the milk produced on the inside of its little bag-like home. After seven weeks the baby leaves the safety of its mother's pouch. Its prickly spines begin to make its mother itch and she is glad to see it go. But the female continues to feed her offspring for several weeks more before it is weaned.

▶ The female koala breeds every other year. The mother usually produces one baby at a time which she carries on her back for a year before it is ready to fend for itself.

From joey to giant

The red kangaroo is the biggest of all marsupials. At 7 feet (2 meters) tall and 176 lb (80 kg) in weight it is a real giant. But it started life much much smaller, less than an ounce in weight. But even such a small baby animal can usually find the strength to climb into its mother's pouch. As soon as it is safely tucked inside, it attaches to a nipple and starts to suck its mother's milk.

▲ A baby kangaroo or joey spends about seven months being carried about by its mother. It gradually begins to climb out to spend more and more time exploring the world outside. But it always returns to the pouch for safe keeping.

▼ When danger threatens, a joey dives back into the pouch head first. It manages to tumble in safely, even if its mother has already started hopping away. But it is not long before the joey has turned round and poked its head out to see where it is going.

Mice and bandicoots

The marsupial mouse is one of the pouchless marsupials. Instead of climbing into their mother's "carrier bag," the babies cling to her fur as she scurries about.

The pouch of the long-nosed burrowing bandicoot is rather unusual. It faces backwards to prevent it filling with soil when the animal digs around.

More about ▷▷ Carrying babies p 46-47

Life support system

The safest place for a baby to develop is inside its mother. Some fish, amphibians, and reptiles keep their offspring inside them and all female mammals give birth to live young. They maintain a kind of life support system which keeps the offspring alive and healthy until they are ready to be born.

Swap shop

A baby mammal develops inside a fluid-filled bag called the amnion in its mother's womb. A thin tube called the umbilical cord connects the baby to a special area on the womb called the placenta. This is a kind of exchange center where the blood streams of the mother and baby swop substances. Food and oxygen enters the baby from the mother's blood while waste materials, like carbon dioxide, pass the other way.

▲ This pregnant cow is beginning to swell, but it is probably carrying only one baby in its womb. Big animals have big babies. Usually, there is not room for more than one baby at a time in the womb. But smaller mammals often have lots of babies.

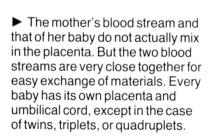

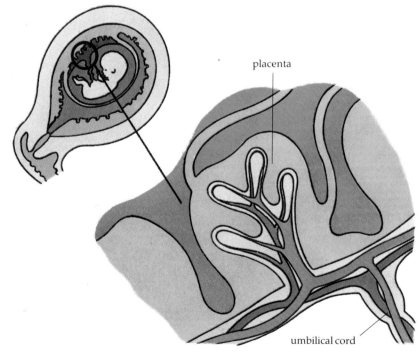

placenta

umbilical cord

▶ The mother's blood stream and that of her baby do not actually mix in the placenta. But the two blood streams are very close together for easy exchange of materials. Every baby has its own placenta and umbilical cord, except in the case of twins, triplets, or quadruplets.

developing baby pig

1
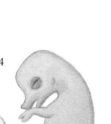

just a few days old

2

2 weeks

3

1 month

4
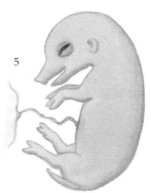

2 months

5
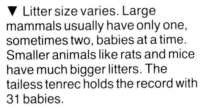

3 months

6
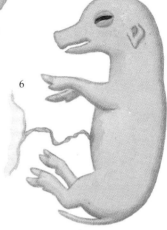

just before birth
at 4 months

▲ After attaching to the womb, a microscopic egg grows very quickly as it receives food from the female's blood. A baby blue whale starts off by weighing only a fraction of a milligram. But it grows into a 3-ton (3-tonne) giant in just over 10 months inside its mother's womb.

▼ Litter size varies. Large mammals usually have only one, sometimes two, babies at a time. Smaller animals like rats and mice have much bigger litters. The tailless tenrec holds the record with 31 babies.

A welcome stay

The length of time a baby mammal spends inside its mother is called the gestation period. In the case of the American opossum this lasts about 12 days. At the other end of scale, a baby Indian elephant waits for as long as 700 days before being born. In general the gestation period is proportional to the size of the mammal. So small mammals like rats and mice have a gestation period of about three weeks while that of a giant like the rhinoceros lasts as long as 550 days.

More about ≫ Blue whale p 39, 41, 52
Birth p 38-39

Being born

Entering the world is one of the most difficult times for any animal. Hungry predators are all around, danger lurks everywhere. Many animals arrive without the help of their parents and they have to move and feed almost immediately. Others are accompanied and helped by one or both parents. The more fully developed the offspring are when they make their arrival, the better their chance of survival.

Fish births

Fish show a wide range of techniques for bringing their offspring into the world. Most do not bother, but some, like the seahorses and mouth brooders, watch over the eggs and babies at the time they arrive on the scene. Some fish even keep their developing offspring inside them and produce them live and fully formed. The spiny dogfish uses this live-bearing technique to produce litters of 3 or 4 young.

▲ Now the eggs have hatched, these tadpoles are in constant danger. They were well protected by the covering of jelly when they were inside the eggs. Now they are free they are easy targets for fish and other predators.

▶ Female bats give birth hanging by all fours in an upside down position. The baby drops into an "apron" formed by the back part of the mother's wing membrane.

Go crack an egg

Most reptiles leave their eggs to hatch by themselves. Once a female green turtle has laid her batches of eggs on a sandy beach it is up to the babies to make their own way into the world. It is not easy for young hatchlings to scramble out of their nest and make a run for it to the water. Young crocodiles do get help from their mother. High-pitched piping calls from the nest tell the female that her babies are beginning to hatch. This sound triggers her to dig away the sand so that the babies can escape.

Ready or not ...

Some baby animals enter the world helpless, naked, and blind. Other animals arrive wide eyed and "fully clothed," ready for action. It all depends how much home life the parents provide. Baby hares are born in the open so they arrive with eyes open and a fur coat. Rabbits build complicated burrows in which their offspring are born. Baby rabbits are much smaller than baby hares when they first enter the world. They are also naked and blind.

Plovers nest in the open so their babies hatch open-eyed and downy. But baby blackbirds are born in a well-built nest. Like baby rabbits, they are born naked with tightly shut eyes.

hare

lapwing

rabbit

blackbird

Beware, water!

Whales and dolphins are born into a watery world so extra care is needed at birth. Usually only a single calf is born to each female. The baby is born tail first. The birth is often attended by a "midwife" who helps the mother to push the baby to the surface to breathe after its connecting cord has been cut by one of the adults in attendance.

▲ Large mammals like wildebeests usually have only one offspring at a time. The baby always gets a glimpse of its new world before the birth is complete. This is because it comes out head and front feet first. A female giraffe gives birth standing up so her baby really does start life with a bang! But it seems to survive its long drop and is soon on its feet and running alongside its mother.

More about ⟫ Fish parents p 28-29 Plovers p 43 Whales p 37, 41, 52
Crocodiles p 23, 44 Tadpoles p 30-31

Mother's milk

All female mammals feed their newly born babies on milk. In many cases the young can be fed in the safety of a den or nest. Even if the parents do not build a home for their offspring, they stay in close contact in the early months for added protection. Because there is always food on tap, baby mammals do not waste energy moving around to look for it. Milk has another advantage. It is an easy liquid to absorb so young mammals do not waste too much energy digesting their food.

▲ Bears usually have only one or two babies and care for them well, rather than going in for mass production. This female is suckling two babies which feed on their mother's milk for several months before being weaned.

▼ Mammary glands develop along two milk lines which run down the female's stomach region. The number of glands is linked to the number of babies in a litter. Pigs may have six pairs of nipples for feeding twelve piglets.

Mammary glands

Different kinds of female mammals have a specific number of mammary glands. The number of nipples depends on how many babies they normally have in a litter. Pigs and dogs produce big litters and because of this they have lots of sucking points or nipples. Elephants and cows have only one baby at a time (sometimes two) so they have only a pair of mammary glands. Each gland is like a bunch of grapes inside. These "grapes" produce the highly nutritious milk for growing babies.

◀ Young dolphins and whales feed on their mother's milk for several months. They drink enormous quantities — a young blue whale calf can drink in one day the same amount of milk as that carried by a fully-loaded milk truck!

Milk make-up

Milk is a very nutritious food. It contains fats, proteins, and sugars. It also contains all the minerals and vitamins a baby needs to make it grow healthy and quickly. It even contains important chemicals which protect the young baby or babies against disease.

The milk content varies between different mammals. In some cases its content changes as the offspring grow older. At the beginning, baby mammals drink a milk which is rich in sugars. Later on the amount of sugar decreases as the milk becomes richer in fats and proteins.

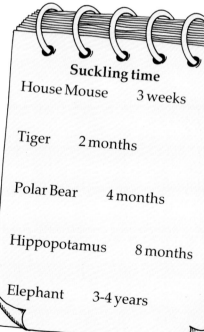

Suckling time

House Mouse	3 weeks
Tiger	2 months
Polar Bear	4 months
Hippopotamus	8 months
Elephant	3-4 years

Female mammals take up different feeding positions. Cows and antelopes stand up to be sucked while rats and mice lie down. The doe hare squats on her back legs and the female rabbit lies on her back. But baby whales have a real problem because they feed in water. The female turns slowly on her side as she swims. As soon as her calf touches a nipple, its mother squirts a huge jet of milk down its throat. This high-pressure hose technique takes only a few seconds each time.

More about ≫ Whales p 39

Protecting the young

Animals often protect their eggs and young. Centipedes curl around their tiny eggs to protect them and small bugs also make good guards. Spiders even spin special cocoons for their babies. Crabs and lobsters carry both eggs and young in a little "pocket" on the abdomen or among bristly hairs on their back legs. However, it is among birds and mammals that we find the most ingenious methods of protecting the young offspring.

▲ In a crowded colony of emperor penguins, parents, and chicks call repeatedly to each other. Probably more than half these babies will live to become adults because of the good protection they get.

▼ This female lion is carrying a baby in her mouth. Many animals move their young to a safer hiding place when danger threatens.

The numbers game

There is usually safety in numbers. Baby animals have a much better chance of survival if they live in groups with older animals. The groups may be herds of large numbers of animals. On the other hand, they may be smaller family units.

Older members of the herd or group often use warning signals to protect their young. Rabbits and some deer flash their white tails as a warning. Thompson's gazelle does a strange jumping dance to alert the whole herd of imminent danger. It is a kind of "watch out" signal.

Decoy parents

Sometimes a parent animal puts its own life in danger protecting its eggs or young from predators. Birds like plovers pretend to be injured in the hope that they appear to be an easier catch! Dragging a "pretend" broken wing, the female leads the predator away from the nest. When she is satisfied that she has lured the predator far enough away, she suddenly flies up and escapes.

▶ Many female mammals defend their young by standing their ground and attacking predators. A pack of hungry hyaenas attempting to snatch a baby black rhinoceros will have to face the fury of its 3-ton (3-tonne) mother!

Look out!

Many animals are able to warn their offspring of approaching danger. Birds are particularly good at this. Sometimes the call is a high-pitched, long whistle. This call warns the young but it does not show the predator where the parent is calling from. On other occasions the alarm call is a series of sharp clicks. Babies also send out their own distress calls if they stray too far and get lost!

Follow that tail!

Animals such as shrews will sometimes form living caravans. The babies follow their mother in single file, each one holding onto the tail of its brother or sister in front. These little caravans are formed only when the family is exploring away from the nest. It may be that hedgehogs and weasels also travel in groups like this.

▶ A family of shrews explores.

More about ⟩⟩ Centipedes p 26, Spiders' eggs p 44
Emperor penguins p 46

Nurseries and crêches

Young animals have a much better chance of survival if they live together in small groups. There is safety in numbers. Baby animals are protected even more if the group has a resident guardian to look after it. Well-guarded nurseries are often used by animals to protect their newborn young.

A dragon guard

The female Nile crocodile lays about 30 or 40 eggs in a shallow pit on the river bank. As soon as they are laid, the eggs are covered with sand and left to incubate. The female makes a frightening guard as she sleeps close by the nest, waiting for the eggs to hatch. About 90 days later, the babies begin to call their mother from inside the eggs. The female hears them and quickly digs the babies out of the sand to start their new life.

As each baby is "rescued," its mother carries it in a special brood pouch in her mouth to the safety of a nearby nursery pool. Here the baby crocodiles remain for about six months under the watchful eye of their mother.

▶ A female crocodile guards both her eggs and young.

▲ The female nursery spider carries her eggs around in a silk purse. Her egg-bag is often so big that she has to walk on tiptoe to keep it off the ground. When the eggs are ready to hatch, the female spins a silk tent in which to place her egg container. The baby spiderlings quickly hatch out in their silken nursery where they remain, guarded by their mother until their first molt.

Tree tadpoles

High up in the rainforest canopy is not the easiest place to find standing water. But small pools do exist, especially in the water-filled hollows of leafy plants. These rainwater leaf cups make perfect nursery ponds for the tadpoles of some arrow poison frogs. Once a female has placed a tadpole in each leafy pool, she visits each in turn and adds a few unfertilized eggs to provide food for her babies. Each rainwater cup acts both as nursery and larder alike.

▲ Baby ducks and goslings are often herded into nursery groups guarded by several adults who are not their parents. Some duck nurseries may contain more than 100 ducklings.

Nursery schools

Many fish, like the jewel fish, keep their babies in nursery schools. When the parents relieve each other, they have a special way of changing guard. One parent swims quickly towards the nursery and then starts zigzagging. This attracts the attention of the nursery. While the babies are looking the other way, the other parent darts off duty. The nursery school carries on as normal but this time under the watchful eye of a new guard.

Giraffe sitters

Giraffe mothers hand their babies over to a "kindergarten" when they are only a few months old. Each crèche group contains four or five calves which are still being suckled by their mothers. The "aunts" look after the calves while their mothers wander away to feed. Their long necks and excellent eyesight make it easy for the mothers to spot the nursery groups from a long way off and quickly find their way back.

More about ⟩⟩
Crocodiles p 23, 38, Spiders p 9, 19 Tadpoles p 30-31, 38
Fish parents p 28-29, Ducklings p 51

Pick-a-back

Many baby animals get a "piggy back" from one or other of their parents or hitch a lift in some other way. Baby animals soon get cold unless they are kept close to their mother's body, so when the female goes looking for food, she takes her family with her.

Young animals also find themselves being carried about when danger threatens. Dogs and cats gently lift their offspring by the scruff of their necks. Bears take the whole of the baby's head into their mouths before setting off.

▲ Newly hatched scorpions climb onto their mother's back. The female sometimes turns her large pincers sideways and rests them on the ground to make a ramp for her babies to climb up. After the first molt, the babies jump off and go their own way.

▲ The male emperor penguin incubates his mate's egg on his feet during the Antarctic winter. The baby is even carried for several weeks as foot passenger after hatching.

Monkey business

Monkeys and apes carry their young from place to place. Sometimes the babies cling to the belly of their mother but on other occasions they ride on the female's back. Young gibbons get a firm grip at the top of their mother's leg near her hips. They have to hold on very tight as the female swings through the trees at a tremendous speed.

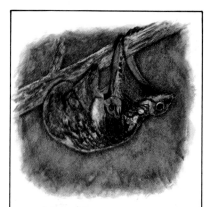

Gliding babies

The colugo is a champion glider. But even when a female is "falling" through space she carries a baby clinging to her nipples or fur. When she hangs upside down to rest, her baby relaxes safely in a natural hammock made by the folds of its mother's large gliding membranes.

46

red-tailed hawk

American woodcock

water rail

Bird lift

Parent birds will sometimes carry their young away from danger. Some hawks grip their offspring in their powerful talons while birds like the woodcock fly with a young bird held between the thighs. The water rail has a more simple technique. It picks up each baby in turn in its beak and rushes it to safety. Large water birds like swans often carry their babies on their backs. In this way the young do not have to waste their energy trying to keep up with their parents. They are also protected from predatory fish.

▲ Very young bats are carried by their mothers in flight. They cling to nipples or fur with their milk teeth. Usually bats have only one baby at a time. Can you guess why? When the babies are older, the females hang them up in the roost when they go hunting.

Bags of room

Lots of animals have special bags or pouches for carrying their young. Some frogs and toads have pits and "zipper bags" and marsupials have pouches. Eggs and babies are sometimes kept in throat sacs and, in the case of one frog, even in the stomach. However, fish have none of these things but the mouth is a natural carrier bag and mouth brooder fish put it to good use.

▲ Like all anteaters, the tamandua carries its young piggy-back fashion. The baby scaly anteater or pangolin has a different technique. It sits astride its mother's tail like a small jockey.

More about ⟩⟩ Protecting the young p 42-43 Emperor penguins p 42 Baby apes p 49
Baby birds p 43 Marsupials p 34-35 Bats p 38

Playtime

Young mammals spend their early months mainly doing three things — feeding, sleeping, and playing. You have probably watched a kitten or puppy chasing its own tail or chasing a piece of paper blowing in the wind. Play is very important to young animals. It helps them develop strong muscles and it begins to train them in developing some of the skills they will use when they are adults. Baby animals wrestle with each other and pretend at scratching and biting. But they never really hurt one another. Sometimes they have mock races, play tag, "follow my leader," and even "king o' the castle".

▲ These young foxes are gaining strength by exercising their muscles during play. They often have mock battles with each other when they tumble about.

Invitation to play

Animals often give signals when they want to play. They sometimes show special facial expressions or will stand, squat, or bend in unusual positions. All of these actions say to other animals "I want to play." An adult lion shows a cub it wants to play by sticking its bottom up in the air. Young monkeys bend over and look at their playmates from between their back legs. It is all good fun!

chimpanzee play face

Slipping and sliding

Young otters enjoy a good slide on a wet, muddy river bank or down an icy slope in winter. Even adults are easily tempted to take part in these "fun runs." Adélie penguins also seem to enjoy the feeling of speed when they turn themselves into little toboggans on the ice of their Antarctic home.

Playing with food

It is not only young mammals that play. Even adults join in the "fun" from time to time. Meat-eaters like cats often play with a victim they have caught before finally deciding to eat it. Dolphins behave in a similar way, often catching, releasing, and then re-catching a fish before swallowing it.

Aping around

Some of the most interesting examples of playing have been seen in apes like gorillas and chimpanzees. Baby gorillas find all kinds of things to do and play with. They tear off patches of moss from tree trunks and wear them like a flat cap. They have even been seen to wear a bundle of lobelia leaves rather like a sun hat. Baby gorillas dance together in single file, each one holding tightly to the one in front. Young chimpanzees bounce around like small, furry balls.

▲ Cheetah cubs often play a rough and tumble game with their mother. They nibble at her fur and chase her tail for hours on end. They even jump all over her when she is trying to rest. Gradually the mother begins to make use of these playtimes to teach her cubs how to hunt for food.

More about ⟫⟫ Signals p 8-9, 10-11 Monkeys and apes p 46, 48-49, 51 Dolphins and whales p 39, 41, 52

Lessons for living

Many young animals do things without being taught how. A baby fish swims as soon as it hatches from its egg. A young antelope runs with the herd within an hour of being born. Young animals do lots of things by instinct.

However, parents that look after their offspring can also teach important lessons for survival. A mother hen gathers up her chicks when a cat appears. She is beginning to teach them that a cat is dangerous. She also teaches her brood that haystacks and compost heaps are good places to look for food. Her babies learn by watching and copying.

▲ There are thousands of adults and chicks in this colony of terns. Quick recognition is very important. A returning parent calls from the air. Its chicks hear the call and sit up and start looking around. This makes it easier for the parent to find its nest and babies. Tern chicks recognize only their parents' voices. They can even do this when they are still inside the egg. Is this learning or instinct?

Danger signs

Chicks of many birds crouch in alarm when something flies overhead. But as they grow older, they get used to common sights like ducks and soon learn to ignore them. But they still get very worried when a hawk appears above them. A long-tailed hawk and a long-necked duck have a similar shape. But young birds learn to tell the difference.

unfamiliar   becoming familiar   still unfamiliar

◀ When lion cubs are only a few months old, they will begin to accompany their parents on hunting expeditions. They watch while a kill is made and then rush in to join the feast. They learn important hunting skills by watching. After about one year they begin to hunt their own prey. But their mothers stand by to give help if they need it.

Watch that snake!

Learning to recognize food or tell friend from foe can be very complicated. It is especially so for young animals living in a tropical rainforest. They need to learn a great deal from their parents. Young monkeys are frightened of all snakes. But their parents have been taught to tell poisonous snakes from harmless ones. As soon as a baby monkey sees any snake it panics. If the snake is harmless, the mother sits quietly. She may even hold her baby by the tail to make sure it does nothing silly. But if a snake is dangerous, the mother grabs the baby and moves away. A young monkey learns to tell one snake from another by watching and remembering how its mother behaves.

▲ The first thing a duckling or gosling sees after hatching becomes imprinted on its brain. This object is usually the real mother. It is a bit of rapid learning which takes place in the first few hours of life. But if the babies see something else, they accept this as "mother" instead. If a human is "imprinted" the babies follow him or her everywhere he or she goes.

▲ Many birds of prey have to learn to become good hunters but this means they have to become expert fliers first. Their parents teach them by dropping food so that they can practice catching it in mid-air.

More about ⟩⟩ Hens and chicks p 32 Baby monkeys p 48-49
Ducklings p 45 Lion cubs p 42

Time to grow up

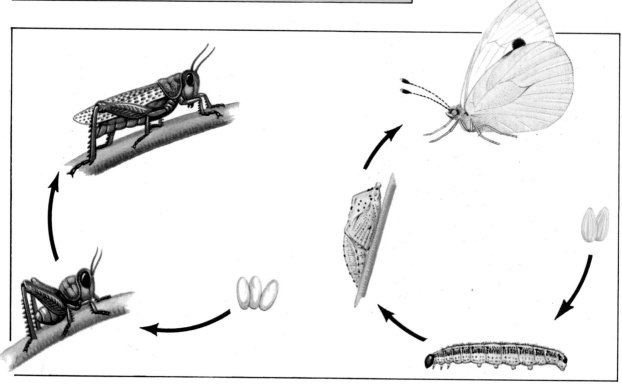

Animals like barnacles and crabs look totally different from their parents as they float around as larvae in the ocean plankton. They change a great deal as they grow older and become adults.

Other animals look similar to their parents at birth. They change mainly in size and proportion. The speed at which baby animals grow varies. The deep-sea clam at 0.3 in (8 mm) in 100 years probably holds the record for the slowest grower. At the other extreme, a blue whale calf wins for speed. The calf increases its weight by about 2.3 tons (2.3 tonnes) in just 18 months after birth!

◄ Insects like grasshoppers hatch, almost like miniature copies of their parents. These larval stages are called nymphs. Each nymph is a feeding and growing stage. Growth takes place by a series of molts when the nymph sheds its skin. After the final molt the grasshopper gets its wings and becomes an adult.

▲ A butterfly goes through a number of stages during its life cycle. Its main feeding stage is when it is a caterpillar. This is also its main growing stage. The remarkable changes that take place inside the pupa are really changes of shape. The adult butterfly is the main, reproductive stage.

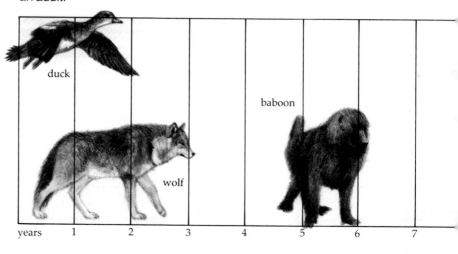

duck

wolf

baboon

years 1 2 3 4 5 6 7

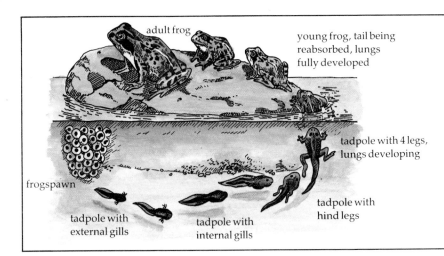

frogspawn

tadpole with external gills

tadpole with internal gills

tadpole with hind legs

tadpole with 4 legs, lungs developing

young frog, tail being reabsorbed, lungs fully developed

adult frog

Frogs and toads change completely during their life cycles. Each egg hatches into a larval tadpole which gradually grows legs and loses its tail. The end result is a froglet or toadlet which looks like a tiny adult. It is now simply a matter of eating and growing bigger. But some salamanders never grow up. They never get beyond the larval stage.

Growing smaller

The paradoxical frog breaks all the rules about growth because it does things the other way round. The tadpoles often measure 10 in (25 cm) in length. But they shrink to produce adults only 2.4 or 2.8 in (6 or 7 cm) long.

◀ A newborn foal looks quite similar to its mother but its body has different proportions. Baby mammals often have outsized heads and legs. They gradually grow to look right.

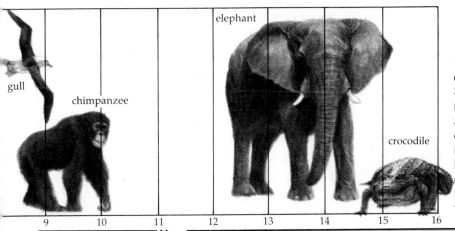

gull

chimpanzee

elephant

crocodile

9 10 11 12 13 14 15 16

◀ The growing up timetable is different for different animals. Smaller animals usually become mature more quickly than big animals. In some cases it may take only a few weeks before an animal is sexually mature and ready to become a parent. But animals like crocodiles and elephants take much longer before they are ready for parenthood.

More about ⟩⟩ Blue whale p 39, 41 Frogs p 30-31 Horses p 14 Crocodiles p 44 Elephants p 15

Happy families

There are an enormous number of different family styles. Many young animals never see their parents. They are orphaned from the time they are in the egg. There are also one parent families where the mother runs the home and the male takes no interest in sharing family duties. Other animals pair up for a breeding season or, in some cases for life. Here both partners take on the responsibility of baby rearing. Then there are the groups, clans, and herds. It is a kind of communal society in which the young are brought up in the company of a number of adults.

▼ Baboons live in troops led by a few dominant males. These and the ordinary males give plenty of protection to the females and babies. A new baby is always an important event and it gets plenty of attention from the troop. Even the males are interested in the babies' arrival.

▲ After mating, a female polar bear goes off by herself to have her babies. The cubs are born in a cosy den under deep drift snow. It is a single parent family where the young stay with their mother for about two years.

Mothers into fathers

There are strange goings-on in the families of some cleaner fish. A male always leads a harem of females. But if the leader dies the dominant female in the harem changes sex and takes over. Within a few hours she starts to behave like a male and within a few days, the new leader is courting and spawning as if he had never been a female!

A typical elephant herd is made up of between 20 and 50 individuals. Usually an older cow acts as leader. The members of the herd work like a real community. They take care of each other and stronger elephants help the weaker ones, including the calves. When a new calf is born, other females get in on the act. They often form a circle around the mother and baby, and one "auntie" gives special help. When a herd is on the move, the adults will help the calves over rough ground. They use their tusks and trunks to push and pull their babies gently along.

Royal households

A colony of social insects like ants, bees, and termites may contain thousands or even millions of individuals. Most nests have only one egg-laying female, called the queen. All members of the colony are her offspring. The queen controls the activities of the colony by giving out chemical messages.

After the queen has laid her eggs, the worker insects carry them off to various kinds of brood chambers where they are looked after. The larvae are fed by the workers before taking their place in society.

▲ The great hornbill pairs for life. After choosing a suitable tree hole, the female cements herself in with the help of her mate. The male feeds his imprisoned mate during incubation and helps her break out when she and her babies are ready.

Foster parents

Some animals leave the job of caring for their young to foster parents. The female cuckoo lays each of her eggs in the nest of another bird. The color and size of the cuckoo's eggs will trick the foster mother into accepting the new egg as one of her own. The newly-hatched cuckoo chick makes sure of a good feed by throwing all the other eggs out of the nest.

Some insects also use the foster parent technique. Some bumble bees play "cuckoo" in the nests of other bumble bees.

More about ≫ Pairing up p 16 Baboons p 9, 19 Elephants p 15
Termites p 7, 13 Tree holes p 12 Birds' eggs p 24-25, 27

Family quiz

Whose home?

A

B

C

▲ Which animal does each of these homes belong to?

True or false

1. A queen termite can lay as many as 8,000 eggs a day.
2. Baby whales and dolphins are always born head first.
3. A rhinoceros spreads chemical messages from glands on its feet.
4. Male spiders give presents to females just before mating.
5. Most female fish produce only a few eggs during the breeding season.
6. Female giraffes give birth standing up.
7. A baby mammal develops inside the mother in the ovary.
8. Animals like swans pair for life.
9. The nine-banded armadillo always gives birth to twins.
10. An ostrich's nest may contain as many as 30 eggs.

Mixed bag

1. What is a pheromone?
2. Give another name for a baby kangaroo.
3. Name the fluid-filled bag in which a baby mammal develops.
4. What name do we give to a badger's underground home?
5. What is so special about the paradoxical frog?
6. What name do we give to an animal that has both male and female sex organs?
7. What is the name given to the process of hatching eggs by keeping them warm?
8. Name a group of fish which keeps in the mouth the fertilized eggs and babies when hatched.
9. What connects the developing baby mammal to the placenta?

Wendy works in a wildlife safari park where she looks after the orangutans. A female who has just given birth has not got enough milk to feed her baby properly, so Wendy has to feed the youngster by hand. But Wendy has a problem. The little orangutan needs to be fed 1 pint of milk every four hours. Wendy only has a 5-pint jug and a 3-pint jug to measure the baby's milk from a big milk churn. How can Wendy measure 1 pint without wasting any milk?

56

A

B

C

Chimpanzees make all kinds of faces to tell other chimps in the family group what mood they are in. Here are three faces showing a chimpanzee in three different moods. Can you match A, B and C against the feelings of excitement, fear and happiness?

▲ Identify this picture.

Snapshot

A wildlife photographer followed a female animal and her two babies 3 miles (5 km) south and 3 miles (5 km) east. He then eventually got the photograph he wanted after stalking the animals for another 3 miles (5 km), which took him back to the point where he started. What was he following?

Family records

1. Which animal has the longest gestation period?
2. Which animal holds the record for the largest number of babies in a litter?
3. Which animal gives birth to the biggest baby?
4. Which animal has the shortest gestation period?
5. Which fish produces the largest number of eggs in a breeding season?
6. Which bird lays the biggest egg?
7. Which animal produces the biggest sperm packet?

Answers

Answers to family quiz

Whose home?:
A. a harvest mouse's nest,
B. a communal weaver bird's nest,
C. a beaver's lodge.

True or false:
1. true, 2. false, 3. true, 4. true, 5. false, 6. true, 7. false, 8. true, 9. false, 10. true.

Mixed bag:
1. a scent or perfume given out by an animal, 2. a joey, 3. the amnion, 4. a set, 5. it gets smaller as it changes from tadpole to adult, 6. an hermaphrodite, 7. incubation, 8. mouthbreeders, 9. the umbilical cord.

Wendy's problem:
First fill the 3-pint jug. Then pour the 3 pints from this jug into the 5-pint jug. Again fill the 3-pint jug and then pour from it into the partially filled 5-pint jug until it is full. This leaves exactly 1 pint in the 3-pint jug.

Chimpanzee moods:
A. happiness, B. fear, C. excitement.

Identify this picture:
A female scorpion carrying her babies on her back.

Snapshot:
A polar bear! The only place on the Earth's surface where such a route is possible is to start at the North Pole.

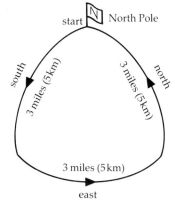

Family records:
1. Indian elephant,
2. tailess tenrec,
3. blue whale,
4. American opossum,
5. ocean sunfish,
6. ostrich,
7. giant octopus.

Glossary

albino: any animal or plant that lacks normal color. Albino animals have whitish hair and pink eyes.

amnion: the bag-like structure in the womb in which the baby mammal develops. It contains a fluid which cushions the developing baby from shock.

breeding season: the time of year when animals mate and have their young.

brood pouch: a patch of almost bare skin on the underside of a bird which covers an egg when the bird is sitting on its nest. There is usually one brood pouch for each egg.

clutch size: the number of eggs laid by a particular kind of bird.

courtship: a special kind of display behavior seen in males and females before mating takes place.

crèche: a group of young animals under the control of one or several adults. The young ones are usually the offspring of several females.

decoy: a trick used by some birds to attract a predator and lead it away from a nest of eggs or young babies.

delayed implantation: the time-lapse between when an egg is fertilized and when it attaches to the wall of the womb. This period can be a number of months in some cases. Bats and bears show this kind of behavior.

egg: a female reproductive cell in an animal or plant.

fertilization: the joining together of a male and female reproductive cell to start the growth of a new animal or plant. The sperm fertilizes the egg.

gestation: the time between fertilization of the egg and the birth of the baby mammal. Small mammals have shorter gestation periods than big mammals.

greeting ceremony: a special kind of behavior shown when two animals meet. Sometimes one animal gives the other animal a present or gift.

harem: a group of female animals belonging to a single dominant male during the breeding season.

hermaphrodite: an animal with both male and female sex organs, e.g. an earthworm.

hypodermic: a hypodermic needle is a fine instrument for injecting fluid under the skin.

incubation: hatching eggs by keeping them warm. The heat may come from the parents' body or the Sun.

imprinting: a piece of rapid learning which takes place in the first few hours of life of a young animal like a duckling or gosling. It is the time when the baby learns to recognize the first object it sees as its mother.

joey: a baby kangaroo.

mammary glands: the structures in the female mammal which produce milk for the newborn young. Different species have different numbers of glands.

marsupial: a mammal whose young are born very small and immature. They spend the early part of their lives in a pouch on the mother's body. Most marsupials live in Australia.

milk lines: the rows of mammary glands on a female mammal.

parthenogenesis: the act of producing offspring without eggs being fertilized by sperms.

pheromones: a chemical with a strong scent sent out by an animal. It affects the way other animals behave.

placenta: the organ in the wall of the womb where the bloodstreams of mother and baby exchange materials.

semaphore: a way of signaling using different positions of the arms to represent letters.

set: a badger's home underground.

spawning: the laying of eggs by fish and amphibians in water.

sperm: the male reproductive cell in an animal.

suckling: the act of a baby mammal feeding on its mother's milk.

territory: an area of space held by an animal and used for breeding. Males establish territory, usually at the beginning of the breeding season.

umbilical cord: the soft cord that joins the developing baby mammal to the mother's placenta.

Index

Acknowledgments

ARTISTS:

Dawn Brend; Adam Hook/Linden Artists; Steve Lings/Linden Artists; Mick Loates/Linden Artists; Alan Male/Linden Artists; Sallie Alane Reason; John Rignall/Linden Artists; Paul Tipper; Terry Burton/Linden Artists; BLA Publishing Limited

PHOTOGRAPHIC CREDITS:

t = top; b = bottom; c = centre; l = left; r = right.

COVER: Seaphot 6 Jonathan Scott/Seaphot. 7 Anthony Bannister/NHPA. 8 W. Wisniewski/Frank Lane Picture Agency. 9 Silvestris/Frank Lane Picture Agency. 10t F. Saure/NHPA. 10b Trevor J. Hill. 11 Leonard Lee Rue/Bruce Coleman Ltd. 12t John Markham/Bruce Coleman Ltd. 12b Peter Johnson/NHPA. 14 Eric Hosking. 14b W. Wisniewski/Frank Lane Picture Agency. 15 Jonathan Scott/Seaphot. 16 Frans Lanting/Bruce Coleman Ltd. 17t Frank Lane Picture Agency. 17b Howard Platt/Seaphot. 18 John Kenfield/Bruce Coleman Ltd. 19t H.D. Brandl/Frank Lane Picture Agency. 19b K & K Ammann/Seaphot. 20 D.J. Patterson/Seaphot. 21 Jane Burton/Bruce Coleman Ltd. 22 Kim Taylor/ Bruce Coleman Ltd. 23 E.A. James/NHPA. 26t C.B. & D.W. Frith/Bruce Coleman Picture Ltd. 26b F.H. Wylie/Frank Lane Picture Agency. 30t H.D. Brandl/Frank Lane Picture Agency. 30b M.P.L. Fogden/Bruce Coleman Ltd. 32 Hans Reinhard/Bruce Coleman Ltd. 33t Lee Lyon/Bruce Coleman Ltd. 33b Roger Wilmshurst/Bruce Coleman Ltd. 34 Karin Cianelli/NHPA. 35 Vincent Serventy/Seaphot. 36 John Lythgoe/Planet Earth Pictures. 37 E. Schuiling/Frank Lane Picture Agency. 38 Stephen Dalton/NHPA. 39 Jonathan Scott/Seaphot. 40t Leonard Lee Rue/Bruce Coleman Ltd. 40b Brian Hawkes/NHPA. 41 Marineland/Frank Lane Picture Agency. 42t A.N.T./ NHPA. 42b Jonathan Scott/Seaphot. 43 Jonathan Scott/Seaphot. 44 John Shaw/Bruce Coleman Ltd. 45 S. Nielson/Bruce Coleman Ltd 46 Stephen Dalton/NHPA. 47 A.N.T./NHPA. 48 Jane Burton/Bruce Coleman Ltd. 49 Fritz Poiking G.D.T./Frank Lane Picture Agency. 50 Anup Shah/Planet Earth Pictures. 51t Jonathan Scott/Seaphot. 51b Jonathan Scott/Planet Earth Pictures. 53 Ray Bird/Frank Lane Picture Agency.